T0022698

Would you like to know Who Created the World?

With acknowledgement and thanks to
Shirley Jackson and Anne Steele

Text and illustrations copyright © 2023 Eira Reeves
This edition copyright © 2023 Lion Hudson IP Limited

The right of Eira Reeves to be identified as the author and illustrator of this work has been asserted by her
in accordance with the Copyright, Designs and Patents Act 1988.

All rights reserved. No part of this publication may be reproduced or transmitted in any form or by any
means, electronic or mechanical, including photocopy, recording, or any information storage and retrieval
system, without permission in writing from the publisher.

Published by **Candle Books**
Part of the SPCK Group
SPCK, Studio 101, 16-16A Baldwins Gardens, EC1N 7RJ London

ISBN 978 1 78128 421 6

First edition 2023

Acknowledgments
Scripture quotations on pages 7, 9, 10, 11, 12, 13, 15, 16–17, 18, 20, 21, 22, 23, 24–25, 26, 27, 29, 32 taken
from the Holy Bible, New International Version®, NIV®. Copyright © 1973, 1978, 1984, 2011 by Biblica,
Inc.™ Used by permission of Zondervan. All rights reserved worldwide. www.zondervan.com
The "NIV" and "New International Version" are trademarks registered in the United States Patent and
Trademark Office by Biblica, Inc.®

Scripture quotations on pages 14, 30, 31 are taken from the Holy Bible, New Living Translation, copyright
©1996, 2004, 2015 by Tyndale House Foundation. Used by permission of Tyndale House Publishers,
Carol Stream, Illinois 60188. All rights reserved.

Scripture quotation on page 28 taken from The Message. Copyright © by Eugene H. Peterson 1993, 1994,
1995, 1996, 2000, 2001, 2002. Used by permission of NavPress Publishing Group.

Scripture on pages 8 and 19 taken from The Voice™. Copyright © 2012 by Ecclesia Bible Society.
Used by permission. All rights reserved.

A catalogue record for this book is available from the British Library

Printed and bound in China, 2023, LH54

Produced on paper from sustainable sources

Would you like to know Who Created the World?

Written and illustrated
by Eira Reeves

CANDLE
BOOKS

Have you ever wondered who created the world...

... and who brought light and life upon the earth?

But God made the earth by his power;
he founded the world by his wisdom.

Jeremiah 10 verse 12

Dear Lord, thank you for creating
everything and giving me joy. Amen

Have you looked at the sky today?

What swirls and patterns can you see in it?

Have you ever thought
who made the clouds
that move around?

 God called the vast expanse "sky".
Genesis 1 verse 8

 Dear Lord, thank you for all the
different shades of light in the sky.
Thank you for the clouds, too. Amen.

Have you ever thought who made the moon and stars?
The moon and stars give some light in the night.

Have you ever tried
to count the stars?

 God made... the lesser light to govern
the night. He also made the stars.
Genesis 1 verse 16

 Dear Lord, I love how you change the
shape of the moon, and you created the
stars to light up the night-time. Amen.

Have you ever wondered about a sunrise
and the beginning of a new day?

What do you do
first when you get
out of bed?

 God called the light "day".
Genesis 1 verse 5

 Dear Lord, I will try to pray to you at
the beginning of a new day. Please help
me to do this. Amen.

Have you watched the sun going down in the evening?
Did it look wonderful, or perhaps it was hidden by clouds?

 ... and the darkness he called "night". And there was evening, and there was morning.

Genesis 1 verse 5

 Dear Lord, Thank you for sunsets. This is the time when I know I will soon go to bed and sleep. Amen.

Have you ever wondered where the rain comes from?

splash... splash... drizzle... drizzle

What do you like
about the rain?
What don't you like?

 He gives showers of rain
to all people.
Zechariah 10 verse 1

 Dear Lord, help me to keep dry in
the rain. Help those people who are
affected by pouring rain that they will
also have shelter. Amen.

Have you ever wondered about thunder and lightning?
How does thunder and lightning make you feel?

rumble... rumble... flash... flash

 His lightning lights up the world.
Psalm 97 verse 4

 Dear Lord, help me not to be frightened
of the thunder and lightning. Amen.

Have you ever wondered how a rainbow appears in the sky?

Can you paint one?

 When I send clouds over the earth, the rainbow will appear in the clouds.

Genesis 9 verse 14

 Dear Lord, I love to see a rainbow. I get excited when I see one. Amen.

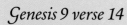

Have you ever seen the snow and how pretty
it is when it first comes down from the sky?

brrrr... brrrr... shiver... shiver

What do you wear
when the weather
is cold?

 He spreads the snow like wool and
scatters the frost like ashes.
Psalm 147 verse 16

 Dear Lord, thank you for the snow in
countries where it falls, and please help
people to keep warm. Amen.

Have you ever wondered who created
the different times of year?

 As long as the earth endures, seedtime and harvest, cold and heat,
summer and winter, day and night will never cease.
Genesis 8 verse 22

Which season do you like and why?

Dear Lord, I love the variety of all the different times of year.
Sometimes the weather is cold and sometimes it is hot.
You created all the seasons to enjoy. Thank you. Amen.

Have you ever thought about water?

ripple... ripple... swirl... swirl

Have you ever paddled in water?
Did it feel good?

 He leads me beside quiet waters.
Psalm 23 verse 2

 Dear Lord, thank you for creating all the lakes, and rivers, and oceans around the world. Amen.

Have you ever wondered who controls the stormy water?

whoosh... whoosh... whoosh

What do you think it would be like to
see big waves crashing onto a beach
and to walk through the wind?

 When you face stormy seas,
I will be there with you.
Isaiah 43 verse 2

 Dear Lord, thank you that you are in
control of all the water around the world
— when it is still and calm, and when it is
stormy. Amen.

Have you ever wondered who made
the mountains, and hills, and fields?

Do you like to walk and run through grass?

 I lift up my eyes to the mountains –
where does my help come from?
My help comes from the LORD.
Psalm 121 verse 1–2

 Dear Lord, thank you for all the fun
and joy we can have in the countryside.
Amen.

Do you know who created the trees?
Do you like to go for walks in the park
or woods and look at the trees?

Have you ever helped to plant a tree?

 The Lord God made all kinds of trees
grow out of the ground – trees that were
pleasing to the eye and good for food.
Genesis 2 verse 9

 Praise to you, Lord, for all the
beautiful trees you created. Amen.

Have you ever wondered who made all the different
fish in the oceans and rivers?

swish... swish... swirl... swirl... swish... swirl

Which ones do you like?

 And God said, "Let the water
teem with living creatures."
Genesis 1 verse 20

 Dear God, I am amazed at all the
creatures around the world, including
fish of all sizes and shapes. Amen.

Have you ever stopped to look at flowers?
Some flowers smell beautiful and look very pretty too.

sniff... sniff... sniff

Who would you like to give a bunch of flowers to?

 God said, "I give you every seed-bearing plant on the face of the whole earth."
Genesis 1 verse 29

 I love all the flowers you have created, God, and you have given them to us to take care of. Amen.

Have you ever wondered where all our food comes from?

munch... munch... yum... yum... gulp... gulp

There is a lot of food in our country, but some countries don't have enough. We need to give them more food.

So whether you eat or drink, or whatever you do, do it all for the glory of God.
1 Corinthians 10 verse 31

 Thank you, dear Lord, for all the food in the world. Help us to share our food with people who do not have much. Amen.

Have you ever thought about how many different
birds there are in the world?

chirp... chirp... tweet... tweet... swoop... swoop

Which birds do you like best?

 Look at the birds of the air; they
do not sow or reap... and yet your
heavenly Father feeds them.
Matthew 6 verse 26

 Dear God, I love to watch all the birds
in the park or gardens as they fly, sing,
and build nests. Amen.

Have you ever wondered how many different animals there are in the world?

moo... moo... snort... snort... baa... baa

Which ones can you name?

 God made the wild animals according to their kinds... And God saw that it was good.
Genesis 1 verses 25

 Dear God, thank you for giving us all the animals – the furry ones, the spiky ones, the big ones and the small ones – for us to enjoy. Amen.

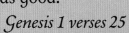

Have you ever thought about how people
around the world speak different languages?

Hello... Halo... Shalom... Bonjour

Can you speak another language?

 Kind words heal and help.
Proverbs 15 verse 4

 Dear God, thank you that we can
speak different languages in so many
countries. Help me always to say kind
words. Amen.

Do you wonder sometimes where you come
from and how you came into the world?
God created you and you are special.

 For you created my inmost being;
you knit me together in my
mother's womb.

Psalm 139 verse 13

 Dear God, thank you for creating me so
beautifully. I am so special in your eyes.
Amen.

Have you ever wondered about the different feelings
we have been given by God? Sometimes we cry.
Sometimes we laugh. Sometimes we comfort others,

and sometimes we dance with joy.

 Be happy with those who are happy,
and weep with those who weep.
Romans 12 verse 15

 Dear God, thank you that you are
always with us. You are with us when
we are happy, sad, rejoicing, dancing,
or comforting someone. Amen.

Do you ever wonder where love comes from?
Who would you like to hug today?
Love is very special for special
people in your life.

 See how very much our Father loves us, for he calls us his children, and that is what we are!

1 John 3 verse 1

 Dear Heavenly Father, thank you for all your precious love you give us. I would like to tell you how much I love you. Amen

Do you wonder about how God has given us so much in the world?
A world that He has created for us so that we can enjoy everything.

We need to take care of all
that He has made.

 I will give thanks to you, LORD, with all my heart; I will tell of all your wonderful deeds.
Psalm 9 verse 1

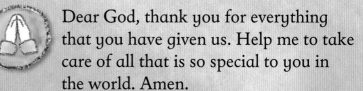 Dear God, thank you for everything that you have given us. Help me to take care of all that is so special to you in the world. Amen.